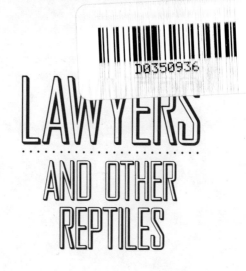

LAWYERS
AND OTHER
REPTILES

LAWYERS

AND OTHER REPTILES

JESS M. BRALLIER

CONTEMPORARY
BOOKS

CHICAGO

Library of Congress
Cataloging-in-Publication Data

Brallier, Jess M.
    Lawyers and other reptiles / Jess
M. Brallier.
        p.   cm.
    ISBN 0-8092-3919-1 (cloth)
    1. Lawyers—Humor.
    2. Lawyers—Quotations.   I. Title.
    II. Title: Lawyers and other reptiles.
PN6231.L4B68   1992
808.8'2—dc20   91-44987
                                CIP

Published by Contemporary Books, Inc.
Two Prudential Plaza,
    Chicago, Illinois 60601-6790
Manufactured in the United States
    of America
International Standard Book Number:
    0-8092-3919-1

To Max and Ruby

LAWYERS

AND OTHER REPTILES

INTRODUCTION: LIFE AND LAWYERS

. . . .

THE BLISS OF CHILDHOOD

When I was a child and life was sweet, innocent, and full of fun, there were no lawyers. Sure, there was a lawyer's office down the street and one of my friends, Freddy, even had a lawyer for a father. But lawyers weren't *in* my life, not the way that kind and helpful grown-ups like doctors, teachers, police officers, and barbers were. You see, a kid can look, listen, and understand what these normal grown-ups do. But a lawyer?—nah!

And, certainly, in my early childhood none of us actually wanted to grow up to be a lawyer. After all, Freddy's father didn't really *do* anything, and what child dreams of growing up to do nothing? Yes, life was very good then and very much without lawyers.

THE UNCERTAINTY OF ADOLESCENCE

But five to ten years later, life got much more confusing: hormones kicked in; *Highlights* magazine was out, *Newsweek* and *Time* were in; and late-night television was suddenly accessible. It was then that my friends and I first began to read and hear about lawyers. The early indications were not promising—lawyers were always part of "bad" stories like murders and Congress.

And sometimes—now that we were older and our parents weren't so careful with their conversations—that word "lawyer" would be overheard. Mom and Dad said it with a special dreadful tone, just like they said "taxes," "bills," "surgery," "IRS," and "Aunt Clara's visiting for two weeks."

THE REALITY OF ADULTHOOD

Then another four years or so went by and life got even less attractive—it was at last time to grow up. Suddenly, all sorts of friends, relatives, and even girl-friends were becoming lawyers. They started talking funny, dressing stiffly, and acting weird around the same time horrible adult things like bosses, mort-gages, and sexually transmitted diseases started showing up.

At about this time, halfway through that first truly good martini, one comes to the reali-zation that *life with lawyers is far worse than life without lawyers.*

Life then becomes a never-ending process of reconfirming that martini-inspired thesis. You get divorced and lawyers are there. You ram your little car into a big truck and suddenly lawyers appear. You default on a loan and lots and lots of lawyers get involved.

So what's one to do? Law-yers—you can't live with them and you can't live without them—especially when so many of them are friends, neighbors, brothers, sons, and daughters.

One night, about twenty-two minutes into a really obnoxious episode of "L.A. Law," the an-swer suddenly became crystal clear to me: laugh at them!

Thus, *Lawyers and Other Reptiles*.

"Clinton has conducted the opening weeks of his Presidency in a lawyerly way, getting bogged down in technicalities, loopholes, caveats, and flyspecking."
—*The New York Times*

"The mere title of lawyer is sufficient to deprive a man of the public confidence. . . . The most innocent and irreproachable life cannot guard a lawyer against the hatred of his fellow citizens."
—*John Quincy Adams, 1787*

"I don't know of any other industry, except the movie business, that has so many stars. Every lawyer thinks he's special."

—*Peter Morrison*

"My whole family follows the medical profession closely," said the young man. "They're lawyers."

"Doctors and lawyers must go to school for years and years, often with little sleep and with great sacrifice to their first wives."

—*Roy Blount, Jr.*

"There was a time when an apple a day kept the doctor away, but now it's malpractice insurance."
—*Dr. Laurence J. Peter*

An attorney phoned the governor just after midnight, insisting that he must speak to him regarding a matter of extreme urgency. An aide eventually agreed to wake the governor.

"So what is it?" the governor screamed into the phone.

"Well, Governor," said the attorney, "Judge Williams just died, and I want to take his place."

The governor responded immediately, "It's all right with me if it's all right with the undertaker."

"A man who never graduated from school might steal from a freight car. But a man who attends college and graduates as a lawyer might steal the whole railroad."

—*President Theodore Roosevelt, attempting to persuade his son to become a lawyer*

At a cemetery outside of Buffalo three men—a contractor, a physician, and a lawyer—joined the grieving widow at the services for their dearest friend. The widow asked if each could place an offering in the casket, as this had long been a custom in her husband's family. ▷

The contractor nodded his head and then said a short prayer before placing a hundred-dollar bill in the casket.

The physician, nearly in tears, also placed a hundred-dollar bill in the casket.

Then the lawyer scribbled out a check for three hundred dollars, put it in the casket, and pocketed the two hundred dollars in cash.

"The first thing we do, let's kill all the lawyers."
—*Shakespeare (King Henry the Sixth, Part 2)*

"The lawyer has learned how to flatter his master in word and indulge him in deed; but his soul is small and unrighteous. . . . from the first he has practiced deception and retaliation, and has become stunted and warped. And so he has passed out of youth into manhood, having no soundness in him. . . ."

—*Plato (321 B.C.)*

Lawyers can't go to the beach anymore. Cats keep trying to bury them in the sand.

"As we watched Judge Clarence Thomas's Supreme Court confirmation hearings, all of the commentators said the same thing: 'One of these people in the room is lying.' Do you believe that? You've got two lawyers and 14 senators in the room, and only *one* of them is lying?"

—*Jay Leno*

A guy standing in line at a bank endorsed a check by writing:

X

The man behind him said, "Hey, what's that X mean?"

"That's my signature. It says 'John Smith,' " replied the first man.   ▷

"What a coincidence! I sign my name the same way," said the second man, who proceeded to endorse a check this way:

XXX

"What do those little Xs mean?" asked the first man.

The second man replied, "This says, 'John Smith, attorney-at-law.' "

"It isn't the bad lawyers who are screwing up the justice system in this country—it's the good lawyers. If you have two competent lawyers on opposite sides, a trial that should take three days could easily last six months."
—*Art Buchwald*

When a Cleveland lawyer got an Akron girl pregnant, he actually offered (to the astonishment of his partners) to do the right and proper thing—marry her.

But she refused his proposal. Stunned, the lawyer insisted on knowing why.

Her reply: "Well, my parents may not have much money or schooling but they have their pride. So when I told them about my condition, everyone pretty much felt that it was better to have a bastard in the family rather than a lawyer."

"The trouble with law is lawyers."

—*Clarence Darrow*

"What is the first excellence in a lawyer? Tautology. What is the second? Tautology. What is the third? Tautology."

—*Richard Steel*

A stranger walked up the street of a small Kentucky town until he found someone he thought was surely a native. "Pardon me," the stranger asked, "are you a resident of this town?"

"Yep, have been for forty years. Something I can do for you?"

"I'm looking for a criminal lawyer. Have you got one here?"

"Well, I suppose we do, but we can't prove it on him."

"Lawyers as a group are no more dedicated to justice or public service than a private utility is dedicated to giving light."
— *David Melinkoff, professor, UCLA*

The difference between a porcupine and a Porsche with two lawyers in it is that the porcupine's pricks are on the outside.

Upon his death in 1869, a French attorney bequeathed $10,000 to "a local madhouse," declaring that "it was simply an act of restitution to his clients."

"He was a lawyer, yet not a rascal, and the people were astonished."

—*anonymous, said of Saint Ives, thirteenth-century lawyer and a saint*

SPANISH PROVERBS

"Win your lawsuit, lose your money."

. . . .

"A peasant between two lawyers is like a fish between two cats."

"If all the lawyers were hanged tomorrow, and their bones sold to a mahjongg factory, we'd be freer and safer, and our taxes would be reduced by almost half."

—*H. L. Mencken*

"A well-known occupational hazard of lawyers is their tendency to become contentious, and to develop such associated traits as being arrogant, deceitful, and punitive."

—*David Riley, attorney and writer*

"The trial lawyer does what Socrates was executed for: making the worse argument appear the stronger."

—*Judge Irving Kaufman*

A prominent Boston physician was vacationing north of Boston near Manchester beach when he wandered into a carpenter's shop. There he was soon intrigued by the wooden sculpture of a rat and inquired as to its availability.

"That damn piece has been brought back to me twice," said the carpenter, "so although it's worth much more, you can have it for five dollars."

The doctor bought the rat ▷

sculpture and continued on his walk. After a bit he noticed several rats scurrying about. Then he noticed more rats. And then suddenly there were hundreds, seemingly thousands, of rats—and they were following him!

Certain that the rats must have something to do with the sculpture, he ran to the harbor and threw the sculpture into the water. Without hesitation, all the rats followed it to their watery death.

Immediately the doctor returned to the carpenter's shop, where he was rebuffed by the owner: "No, no! Now get out of here, sir. I'm not taking that sculpture back!"

"Calm down," said the doctor reassuringly. "I only wanted to know if you might have a sculpture of a lawyer?"

Washington, D.C., has the most lawyers and New Jersey the most toxic-waste dumps because New Jersey had first choice.

"I told you you should've got yourself some legal advice before running to a lawyer." (overheard in a courthouse corridor)
—*The New Yorker*

"The doctor is in court on Tuesdays and Wednesdays."
—*overheard at a doctor's office*

More and more medical laboratories are now using lawyers instead of rats for experimentation because

1. there are more lawyers available
2. rats are better looking
3. lab technicians don't get emotionally attached to lawyers
4. there are some things a rat wouldn't dare do

QUESTION: How many lawyers does it take to screw in a light bulb?
ANSWER: How many can you afford?

"Lawyers are plants that will grow in any soil that is cultivated by the hands of others, and when once they have taken root they will extinguish every vegetable that grows around them. The most ignorant, the most bungling member of that profession will, if placed in the most obscure part of the country, promote litigiousness and amass more wealth than the most opulent farmer with all his toil. . . . What a pity that our forefathers, who happily extinguished so many fatal customs and expunged from their new government so many errors and abuses both religious and civil, did not prevent the introduction of a set of men so dangerous."

—H. St. John Crevecoeur, 1787

"Deals aren't usually blown by principals; they're blown by lawyers and accountants trying to prove how valuable they are."
—*Robert Townsend*

"A man may as well open an oyster without a knife as a lawyer's mouth without a fee."
—*Barten Holyday*

"It is a maxim among these lawyers that whatever hath been done before may legally be done again, and therefore they take special care to record all the de-▷

cisions formerly made against common justice and the general reason of mankind. These, under the name of precedents, they produce as authorities, to justify the most iniquitous opinions. . . ."

—*Jonathan Swift*

"A lawyer is a man who helps you get what is coming to him."
—*Laurence J. Peter*

QUESTION: What does a lawyer use for a contraceptive?
ANSWER: His personality.

DANISH PROVERBS

"Lawyers and painters can soon change white to black."

. . . .

"Virtue down the middle," said the Devil, as he sat down between two lawyers.

A MOST QUICK-WITTED PROFESSION

(the following exchanges actually took place in a courtroom)

COUNSEL: Do you recall approximately the time you examined the body of Mr. Edgington at the Rose Chapel?

WITNESS: It was in the evening. The autopsy started about 8:30 P.M.   ▷

COUNSEL: And Mr. Edgington was dead at that time, is that correct?

. . . .

DEFENDANT: Judge, I want you to appoint me another lawyer.

THE COURT: And why is that?

DEFENDANT: Because the P.D. isn't interested in my case.

THE COURT: (to public defender) Do you have any comments on defendant's motion?

PUBLIC DEFENDER: I'm sorry, Your Honor, I wasn't listening.

. . . .

COUNSEL: Was there some event, Valerie, that occurred which kind of finally made you determined that you had to separate from your husband?

WITNESS: Yes.   ▷

COUNSEL: Did he try to do something to you?

WITNESS: Yes.

COUNSEL: What did he do?

WITNESS: Well, uh, he tried to kill me.

COUNSEL: All right. And then you felt that that was the last straw, is that correct?

. . . .

COUNSEL: Can you participate in an endeavor in which the ultimate result might be death by lethal injection?

POTENTIAL JUROR: Yeah, I guess I could do it if it was on a weekend.

. . . .

COUNSEL: Did you see any feces on the ground?

WITNESS: I didn't see any—I didn't see any fishes.

COUNSEL: Not fishes, feces. ▷

WITNESS: Little frogs. No I didn't see any.

COUNSEL: When you don't pass water, when you do number two.

WITNESS: I don't understand.

COUNSEL: Okay. Pardon me, ladies and gentlemen. Did he take a shit? Did you see any of that?

WITNESS: I didn't see that, no.

COUNSEL: Did you smell it?

WITNESS: Why should I go and smell his shit?

"No poet ever interpreted nature as freely as a lawyer interprets truth."

—*Jean Giraudoux*

A Philadelphia obstetrician—recently divorced and twice sued for malpractice—was in desperate need of a break from all the lawyers, so he went out West for a vacation.

Finding a tavern with a friendly bartender, he began to drown his troubles. After a few drinks, the obstetrician suddenly blurted out, "Goddamn lawyers—what a bunch of horses' asses!"

"Geez, doc," cautioned the bartender, "don't say stuff like that around here—this is horse country."

Undistinguished and often shabby in appearance, Ulysses S. Grant did not recommend himself to strangers by his looks. He once entered an inn on a stormy winter night. A number of lawyers, in town for a court session, were clustered around the fire. One looked up as Grant appeared and said, "Here's a stranger, gentlemen, and by the looks of him he's traveled through hell itself to get here."

"That's right," said Grant cheerfully.

"And how did you find things down there?"

"Just like here," replied Grant, "lawyers all closest to the fire."

GREAT MOMENTS BROUGHT TO US BY LAWYERS

In 1971, an attorney filed suit in Pennsylvania against Satan and his servants, claiming they had placed obstacles in his client's path which caused his downfall.

To the attorney's dismay, the complaint was denied on the grounds that the defendant did not reside in Pennsylvania.

. . . .

An attorney sued a meditation society and its guru because after eleven years, his client still had never achieved the "perfect state of life" they had promised.

For example, he was told he would be taught to "fly" through self-levitation, but he only learned to "hop with the legs folded in the lotus position."

The lawyer secured an award of over $137,000 in damages.

. . . .

When a New York City man tried to commit suicide by throwing himself off a subway platform into the path of an oncoming train, the train stopped and he was only injured. So the guy's lawyer sued the transit authority, claiming that "the motorman was negligent in *not stopping the train quickly enough.*"

The lawyer settled out of court for $650,000, even though in the midst of negotiations his client threw himself off another subway platform, once more failing to kill himself.

· ·

In 1989, after a Long Island man was convicted of murdering his wife's parents and teenage brother, a lawyer convinced the court that his wife should pay her husband's legal fees of more than $100,000.

· ·

"Your spouses are going to change: their personalities are going to change in law school. They'll get more aggressive, more hostile, more precise, more impatient."
—*Soia Mentschikoff,*
  University of Chicago, to the
  wives and husbands of
  first-year law students

A missed opportunity: a busload of lawyers with one empty seat went over a cliff.

EDUCATING AMERICA'S FUTURE LAWYERS

According to the *New York Times*, in July 1990 a new summer camp opened: "National Law Camp: Educating America's Future Lawyers—while other kids are practicing tennis this summer, yours can be practicing law." Campers study torts, evidence, trial advocacy, and ethics. Field trips are to courthouses and jails. And, like the lawyers they long to be, the campers awaken to alarm clocks rather than to reveille.

. . . .

"According to my family, I have this big mouth and I should put it to good use."

> —*Elena Laguardia, on why she's at camp*

. . . .

"I see no point in wasting time. . . . Reading Danielle Steel all summer just doesn't do it."
— *Gigi "little yuppie" Oden, who hopes to be a prosecutor, on why she's at camp*

. . . .

"My mother wants me to be a corporate lawyer because they make more money."
— *Kenyetta Finely, a camper who would rather someday be a prosecutor putting away drug dealers*

. . . .

"To learn torts at thirteen strikes me as premature."
— *Paul D. Carrington, professor, Duke Law School*

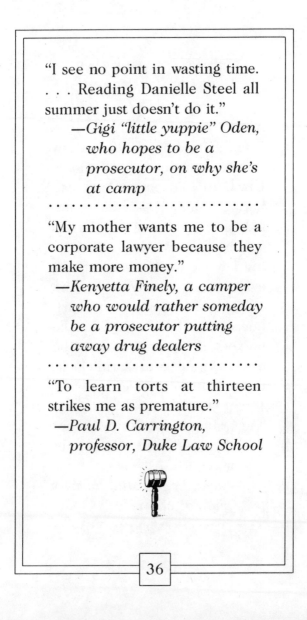

"There is never a deed so foul that something couldn't be said for the guy; that's why there are lawyers."

—*Melvin Belli*

Just before a McKeesport, Pennsylvania, man was found guilty of all charges connected with burning the hands of his three children over a gas stove, his lawyer pointed out to the judge that, after all, "he could have killed them. . . ."

"He committed these acts with love in his heart."

> —*defense attorney Elijah Miller, on John List, who systematically executed his mother, wife, and three children*

"I don't give a shit what happens. I want you to stonewall it, let them plead the Fifth Amendment, cover up, or anything else. . . ."

> —*attorney (and President) Richard M. Nixon to attorney (and Attorney General) John Mitchell, sitting around the White House Oval Office discussing Watergate*

QUESTION: How do you know that God, who created the world out of chaos and darkness, is a lawyer?

ANSWER: Because he made chaos and darkness first.

"It was cheaper than paying lawyers."

—*Robert Vesco, on why he contributed $200,000 to the Committee to Reelect the President (CREEP)*

Then there's the lawyer who in 1980 bragged that while en route from New York to San Francisco to take care of a matter for IBM, he used the airborne hours to work on a General Motors case—and billed *both* IBM *and* General Motors $250 an hour for the time he was airborne.

"It is the trade of lawyers to question everything, yield nothing, and to talk by the hour."
—*Thomas Jefferson*

An elderly, nearly blind woman hired a lawyer to draft her will. When it was completed, the lawyer charged her one hundred dollars. She handed the lawyer a hundred-dollar bill but failed to notice that a second hundred-dollar bill was stuck to it. Immediately the lawyer realized he was faced with a vital ethical question: "Should I tell my partner?"

"They all laid their heads together like as many lawyers when they are gettin' ready to prove that a man's heirs ain't got any right to his property."
—*Mark Twain*

"If you think that you can think about a thing, inextricably attached to something else, without thinking of the thing it is attached to, then you have a legal mind."

—*Thomas Reed Powell*

"The most amazing sensation here since the last amazing sensation here a couple of years ago."

—*Palm Beach, Florida, attorney Charles Senatore, offering his legal insight on the "Kennedy rape case" of 1991*

"When the president does it, that means it is not illegal."
—*attorney Richard M. Nixon*

Two farmers each claimed to own a certain cow. While one pulled on its head and the other pulled on its tail, the cow was milked by a lawyer.
—*Jewish Parable*

"Litigation is the basic legal right which guarantees every corporation its decade in court."
—*David Porter*

The Devil approached a hard-working lawyer and asked, "Aren't you tired of not making all the money you deserve? sick of not being respected like physicians are? frustrated by the long hours?"

"Sure I am," replied the lawyer.

"Just as I thought," said the Devil. "So here's what I'm going to offer you: over a million dollars a year in income, a penthouse in Manhattan, a private jet, an oceanside mansion, a vacation every other week, and your choice of the sexiest women in the world."

The lawyer smiled.

"And in return," the Devil continued, "all I ask is for your eternal soul."

The lawyer paused to give the offer serious consideration. He▷

played with his suspenders, he fingered an unlit cigar, and ignored the scream of an ambulance passing by outside. He eyed the Devil. He concentrated. Then he sighed, "OK, what's the catch?"

"God works wonders now and then;
Behold! a Lawyer, an honest Man."
   —*Benjamin Franklin, 1733*

In 1988, a defense attorney appealed his client's conviction, protesting that a Tuolumne County (Calif.) assistant district attorney disrupted trial proceedings by passing gas—"He farted about one hundred times. . . . He even lifted his leg several times!"

There are more lawyers just in Washington, D.C., than in all of Japan.

"They've got about as many lawyers as we have *sumo* wrestlers."
   —*Lee Iacocca, on the lack of litigation among Japanese businesses*

LAWYERS AT THEIR VERY BEST

A Los Angeles man was extremely upset when he failed the state bar exam. So he allegedly coerced his seven-months' pregnant wife to dress in men's clothing and take the bar exam under his name. She took the test, did well enough to achieve the ninth-highest score in the state, then went immediately to the hospital to give birth to her premature daughter. The man thereupon abandoned his wife and child. The California State Supreme Court later disbarred the wife for her role in the charade.

QUESTION: How do you know when a lawyer is lying?
ANSWER: His lips move.

The doctor finally reached his table at a dinner after breaking away from a woman who sought advice on a health problem.

"Do you think I should send her a bill?" the doctor asked a lawyer who sat next to him.

"Why not?" the lawyer replied. "You rendered professional services by giving advice."

"Thanks," the physician said. "I think I'll do that."

When the doctor went to his office the next day to send a bill to the woman, he found a note from the lawyer. It read:

"For legal services, $50."

In 1990, Dr. James M. Dabbs, Jr., a psychologist with Georgia State University, revealed that high levels of testosterone—which causes overly aggressive or antisocial behavior—is commonly found in juvenile delinquents, substance abusers, rapists, bullies, dropouts, and *trial lawyers.*

In 1985, the official portrait of former inmate John Mitchell was hung at the Justice Department.

A woman fell in love with her divorce lawyer, a married man. "David," she begged, "isn't there some way we can be together?"

Sternly, the lawyer replied, "Gulping drinks in dark bars, hiding out on the wrong side of town, lying to friends and family, meeting on the sly in seedy motel rooms—is that really what you want?"

"No, no," she sobbed, heartbroken.

"Oh," said the lawyer. "Well, it was just a suggestion."

An Ohio man went to see a Cleveland lawyer and asked what his least expensive fee was.

"One hundred dollars for ▷

three questions," said the lawyer.

"Isn't that an awful lot of money for three questions?" asked the man.

"Yes," said the lawyer. "What is your final question?"

As of July 1990, the Manville Personal Injury Settlement Trust was depleted of funds because *lawyer fees consumed 40 percent of the trust*—and this after claim payments were made to only the first 22,386 asbestos workers and their families. As a result, 130,000 more claimants will have to wait *25 years* until the trust refills.

When a Decatur, Georgia, man was charged with having tortured and killed seventy-seven cats, he blamed the matter on stress caused by his failure to pass the state bar examination.

"I've had ample contact with lawyers, and I'm convinced that the only fortune they ever leave is their own."

—*Wilson Mizner*

The priest's friend loses his faith, the doctor's his health, the lawyer's his fortune.

—*Venetian Proverb*

"Lawyers earn a living by the sweat of their browbeating."
—*James Gibbons Huneker*

TALK LIKE A LAWYER! CREATE YOUR OWN LEGAL MUMBO-JUMBO PHRASES! NO LESSONS, NO LAW SCHOOL, NO BAR EXAMINATION! JUST FOLLOW THE INSTRUCTIONS!

Instructions: String together any three words or phrases from List A, List B, and List C. (Helpful Hints: 1. Keep this next to your phone. Use your own legal mumbo-jumbo phrases when the landlord, bill collectors, ex-spouses, or customers call. Better yet, use it when their lawyers phone! Or even when your *own*▷

lawyer calls—if the bum ever returns your message! 2. Don't worry if your legal mumbo-jumbo phrase doesn't make any sense—it just means you have a natural flair for the legal profession. 3. After using a legal mumbo-jumbo phrase, be sure to bill somebody for it—we suggest between $80 and $200.) Example: "hereunder set forth to the contrary"

List A

hereinbefore	foregoing
thereof	breach or
hereunder	alleged
hereof	breach
in the event of	parties of the
person or	first part
entity	

List B

provided	in no event
by and	herein
between	provided,
set forth	however
whatsoever	undersigneds
notwithstanding	

List C

whereas	indemnity
jurisdiction	sole discretion
liens and	including, but
encumbrances	not limited to
shall not	pursuant
breach	
to the	
contrary	

Samuel Johnson (1709–1784) once remarked that "he did not care to speak ill of any man behind his back, but he believed the gentleman to be an *attorney*."

"Why is there always a secret
   singing
When a lawyer cashes in?
Why does a hearse horse snicker
Hauling a lawyer away?"
                    —*Carl Sandburg*

QUESTION: What's black and brown and looks good on a lawyer?
ANSWER: A doberman.

QUESTION: What do you call a hundred lawyers chained together at the bottom of the ocean?
ANSWER: A good start.

"Be frank and explicit with your lawyer. . . . It is his business to confuse the issue afterwards."
—*J. R. Solly*

For years two brothers—one a lawyer and the other a deaf-mute accountant—worked for a mobster. Whenever the mobster and the accountant needed to communicate, the lawyer brother would use sign language and serve as an interpreter.

One day the mobster realized his books were short three million dollars. He called in the two brothers. Looking at the lawyer and pointing to the accountant, he screamed, "You tell this son-of-a-bitch I want to know where my money is!"

The brothers conversed briefly, and the lawyer reported that his brother had no idea what the mobster was talking about.

Furious, the mobster put a gun to the accountant's head and screamed at the lawyer brother, "Tell this bastard that▷

he lets me know—right now—where the damn money is or I'll blow his brains out!"

The lawyer told this to his brother, who immediately explained—in frantic sign language—that the money was hidden in a suitcase under his basement steps.

"Well? What'd he say?" yelled the mobster.

The lawyer shrugged, "He says you don't have the balls."

When a Dublin attorney died in poverty, his legal colleagues set up a fund to pay for his funeral. Upon being solicited, Lord Norbuy (1745–1831), a judge, asked what sum would be appropriate ▷

to contribute. When told that no one else had donated more than a shilling, he exclaimed, "A shilling!" and reached into his pocket. "A shilling to bury an attorney? Why, here's a guinea! Bury one and twenty of the scoundrels."

"Lawyers are like beavers: They get in the mainstream and dam it up."

—*John Naisbitt*

In 1990 an attorney used his own earphones for an in-flight movie instead of renting a set like everyone else. He was arrested as he departed the plane and, of course, soon thereafter began legal action against the airline.

Noted United Airlines official Alan B. Wayne, "it's always interesting that these people are lawyers."

"What's the use of that, Wendell, a lawyer can't be a great man!"
—*Oliver Wendell Holmes, Sr., on his son's plans to attend law school*

A priest, a doctor, and a lawyer were stranded on a boat for days. Starving, the exhausted trio finally neared an island surrounded by shark-infested waters.

Ignoring the obvious danger, the priest began to swim toward the island but was soon eaten by a shark. Next, the doctor began to swim and he, too, was quickly eaten. Then the lawyer dove in, swam through the sharks, and safely reached the island.

One shark turned to another and said, "You ate that priest, and then you ate that doctor. Why didn't you eat the lawyer?"

"Professional courtesy," replied the shark.

"One thing I supplicate, your majesty: that you will give orders, under a great penalty, that no bachelors of law should be allowed to come here [to the New World]; for not only are they bad themselves, but they also make and contrive a thousand iniquities."

> —*Vasco Nuñez de Balboa,*
> *to King Ferdinand V*
> *of Spain, 1513*

"The ideal client is the very wealthy man in very great trouble."

> —*John Sterling*

A noted criminal defense lawyer was making the closing argument for his client accused of murder, although the body of the victim had never been found. The lawyer dramatically turned to the courtroom's clock and, pointing to it, announced, "Ladies and gentlemen of the jury, I have some astounding news. I have found the supposed victim of this murder to be alive! In just ten seconds, she will walk through the door of this courtroom."

A heavy quiet suddenly fell over the courtroom as everyone waited for the dramatic entry.

But nothing happened.

The smirking lawyer continued, "The mere fact that you were watching the door, expecting the victim to walk into this courtroom, is clear proof that▷

you have far more than even a reasonable doubt as to whether a murder was actually committed." Tickled with the impact of his cleverness, the cocky lawyer confidently sat down to await acquittal.

The jury was instructed, filed out, and filed back in just ten minutes with a guilty verdict.

When the judge brought the proceedings to an end, the dismayed lawyer chased after the jury foreman: "Guilty? How could you convict? You were all watching the door!"

"Well," the foreman explained, "Most of us were watching the door. But one of us was watching the defendant, and he wasn't watching the door."

"You can't earn a living defending innocent people."
—*Maurice Nadjari*

"I deserve respect for the things I did not do."
—*Vice President Dan Quayle, on being asked about the ethics of his getting into Indiana University Law School through a special program created for disadvantaged students*

"A lawyer is a learned gentleman who rescues your estate from your enemies and keeps it himself."

—*Henry Broughman*

More than half of the presidents of the United States—a country burdened with huge debt, a devastating crime rate, a failing educational system, excessive acid rain, and an embarrassing series of World Cup performances—have been lawyers.

"The appearance in our courts of these learned gentlemen of the law, who can make black appear white and white appear black, is forbidden."

> —*1864 decree (and still in effect), government of Andorra*

"If the laws could speak for themselves, they would complain of the lawyers. . . ."

> —*Marquis of Halifax*

"Why may not that be the skull of a lawyer? Where be his quiddities now, his quillets, his cases, his tenures, and his tricks?"
—*Shakespeare (Hamlet, Act V, Scene 1)*

A REALLY, REALLY BAD DAY

August 21, 1878: At a meeting in Saratoga, New York, the American Bar Association was founded.

MORE GREAT MOMENTS
BROUGHT TO US BY LAWYERS

In 1989, the lawyer for a Long Island woman who was in prison for having hired a hit man to kill her then husband filed suit against the ex-husband for failing to make monthly support payments. The lawyer argued that just because his client tried to kill the guy, that didn't relieve him of his obligation to support her.

. . . .

In 1964, a woman was injured by a San Francisco cable car. Her lawyer claimed the accident turned her into a nymphomaniac. She won $50,000.

. . . .

Ten years later, in 1974, the same attorney struck again with another client—he sued a health ▷

club for $1 million because his client, after being trapped in a sauna for ninety minutes, became compelled to pick up twenty-four men in barrooms.

. . . .

In 1978, the attorney representing a convicted murderer sued the state of Indiana for transfer to a women's prison on the grounds that his client's sentence of life imprisonment in an all-male prison was cruel and unusual punishment because it imposed upon him a lifetime of celibacy.

"Law reform is far too serious a matter to be left to the legal profession."

—*Leslie Scarman*

Lawyer: 1. A person who takes this from that, with the result that That hath not where to lay his head. 2. An unnecessary evil. 3. The only man in whom ignorance of the law is not punished.

> —*Elbert Hubbard,* The Roycroft Dictionary and Book of Epigrams

He saw a lawyer killing a viper
On a dunghill hard by his own
    stable;
And the Devil smiled, for it put
    him in mind
Of Cain and Abel.
> —*Samuel Taylor Coleridge*

"Divorce is a game played by lawyers."

—*Cary Grant*

"Marriage is really tough because you have to deal with feelings and lawyers."

—*Richard Pryor*

"You're an attorney! It's your duty to lie, conceal and distort everything, and slander everybody!"

—*Jean Giraudoux*

> "Estates should be left to loved ones, not attorneys."
> —*Walter Heiden*

A WATERGATE MINIQUIZ

Which of the following Watergate thugs were lawyers?

a. Richard Nixon
b. John Mitchell
c. Spiro Agnew
d. G. Gordon Liddy
e. John Dean
f. Charles Colson
g. Robert Mardian
h. Herbert Kalmbach
i. John Ehrlichman
j. Donald Segretti

Answer: a, b, c, d, e, f, g, h, i, j

"The worst of law is that one suit breeds twenty."
—*George Herbert, 1593–1633*

A lawyer stepped in some cow dung and thought he was melting.

In Montana, a law student who recently flunked out of law school because she failed her constitutional law course sued, claiming that the school's action was unconstitutional.

"The law is a sort of hocus-pocus science that smiles in your face while it picks your pocket."
—*H. L. Mencken*

One-third of the $25 billion awarded each year in liability lawsuits goes to the lawyers.

When an elderly New York lawyer, after a typically long life of sin, was told he had only days to live, he rushed home and began to frantically leaf through the Bible, looking for loopholes.

The world's record for the most footnotes in a law review article is 4,824.

AND WE'RE SURE THE DEFENSE ATTORNEY HAD NOTHING TO DO WITH IT. . .

In 1928, a San Francisco jury was indicted for destroying evidence in a Prohibition case, having consumed the prosecution's key exhibit.

"A lawyer's dream of heaven—every man reclaimed his property at the resurrection, and each tried to recover it from all his forefathers."

—*Samuel Butler*

Research has confirmed that the best way to drive a lawyer nuts is to squander away all your money without getting him involved.

"I am one of that vast body of loyal, devoted, red-blooded American cynics who despise lawyers as they despise no other ▷

class of fauna. . . . The three times I was most deceived and most poorly served were when I allowed my affairs to go into the hands of officers of the court, sworn to protect my interests. . . . My experience led me to the belief, doubtless mistaken, that most lawyers are swine. And not even nice swine."

—*Charles McCabe,* San Francisco Chronicle

"I don't think you can make a lawyer honest by an act of legislature. You've got to work on his conscience. And his lack of conscience is what makes him a lawyer."

—*Will Rogers*

"If they ever give you a brief, attack the medical evidence. Remember, the jury's full of rheumatism and arthritis and shocking gastric troubles. They love to see a medical man put through it."

—*John Mortimer, advising law students*

When in 1988 a Tucson attorney wore green tennis shoes in the courtroom, the offended judge slapped the dapper lawyer with a 40-hour jail sentence.

PROGRESS ON THE LEGAL FRONT

In 1971, 23 percent of Yale Law School graduates took jobs in the public sector; in 1986, 6 percent did.

When Ravalli County, Montana, fined itself $350 because one of its truck drivers committed a loading violation, it paid the local lawyers hired to prosecute and defend the county $1,175.

STUFF LAWYERS LOVE TO WRITE!

The following was a provision in Citibank's standard loan agreement:

> In the event of default in the payment of this or any other Obligation or the performance or observance of any term or covenant contained or agreement evidencing or relating to any Obligation or any Collateral on the Borrower's part to be performed or observed; or the undersigned Borrower shall die; or any of the undersigned become insolvent or make an assignment for the benefit of creditors; or a petition shall be filed by or against any of the undersigned under any provision of the Bankruptcy Act; or any money, securities ▷

or property of the undersigned now or hereafter on deposit with or in the possession or under the control of the Bank shall be attached or become subject to distraint proceedings or any order of process of any court; or the Bank shall deem itself to be insecure, then and in any such event, the Bank shall have the right (at its option), without demand or notice of any kind, to declare all or any part of the Obligations to be immediately due and payable, whereupon such Obligations shall become and be immediately due and payable, and the Bank shall have the right to exercise all the rights and remedies available to a secured party upon default under the Uniform Commercial Code (the "Code") in effect in New ▷

York at the time, and such other rights and remedies as may otherwise be provided by law. Each of the undersigned agrees (for purpose of the "Code") that written notice of any proposed sale of, or of the Bank's election to retain, Collateral mailed to the undersigned Borrower (who is hereby appointed agent of each of the undersigned for such purpose) by first-class mail, postage prepaid, at the address of the undersigned Borrower indicated below three business days prior to such sale or election shall be deemed reasonable notification thereof. The remedies of the Bank hereunder are cumulative and may be exercised concurrently or separately. If any provision of this paragraph shall conflict with ▷

any remedial provision contained in any security agreement or collateral receipt covering any Collateral, the provisions of such security agreement or collateral receipt shall control.

In 1977, over the extreme reluctance and resistance of its lawyers, Citibank rewrote the above provision (384 words) to read as follows (31 words):

"*Default*: I'll be in default:

1. If I don't pay an installment on time; or
2. If any other creditor tries by legal process to take any money of mine in your possession."

"Lawyers, I suppose, were children once."

—*Charles Lamb*

"When there's a rift in the lute, the business of the lawyer is to widen the rift and gather the loot."

—*Arthur Garfield Hays*

"If a man dies and leaves his estate in an uncertain condition, the lawyers become his heirs."

—*Edgar Watson Howe*

"Bless those men in black robes. They're in the same union with us."

—*Melvin Belli, on judges*

"While law is supposed to be a device to serve society, a civilized way of helping the wheels go round without too much friction, it is pretty hard to find a group less concerned with serving society and more concerned with serving themselves than the lawyers."

—*Fred Rodell, Yale University Law School*

"More lawyers live on politics than flies on a dead camel."
—*Tammany Hall saying*

At a county fair, a musician, a doctor, and a lawyer met at the dog competition and began to argue over whose dog could perform the best trick. The crowd which soon gathered urged the three to conduct a contest to decide the argument.

And so it was agreed.

The musician's dog went first. He masterfully played the piano for five minutes, including selections from Mozart, Handel, and Beethoven. The crowd cheered his performance, and the dog was awarded with a biscuit. ▷

The doctor's dog then performed a successful appendectomy on a stray cat. The doctor's dog was also roundly applauded by the grateful crowd and awarded two biscuits.

"Your turn, boy," said the lawyer, whose dog screwed the other two dogs, took their biscuits, and went out to lunch.

"The problem is not that you can buy a congressman for $10,000 but that you can buy a Washington lawyer for $100,000."
—*former FCC commissioner Nicholas Johnson*

"The Holocaust was an obscene period in our nation's history. I mean this century's history. But we all lived in this century. I didn't live in this century."
—*Dan Quayle, attorney*

"They have no lawyers among them for they consider them as a sort of people whose profession it is to disguise matters."
—*Sir Thomas More, 1516*

"That meanness, that infernal knavery, which multiplies need-less litigations, which retards the▷

operation of justice, which, from court to court, upon the most trifling pretence, postpones trial to glean the last emptyings of a client's pocket, for unjust fees of everlasting attendance, which artfully twists the meaning of law to the side we espouse, which seizes unwarrantable advantages from the prepossessions, ignorance, interests, and prejudices of a jury, you will shun rather than death or infamy."

—*Timothy Dwight, president of Yale College, addressing the graduating class of 1776*

QUESTION: What would you do if you found yourself in a room with Hitler, Mussolini, and a lawyer, and you had a gun with only two bullets?
ANSWER: Shoot the lawyer twice.

It was so cold that a lawyer had his hands in his own pockets.

"Apologists for the profession contend that lawyers are as honest as other men, but this is not very encouraging."
—*Ferdinand Lundberg*

"Many of the most influential and most highly remunerated members of the bar in every center of wealth make it their special task to work out bold and ingenious schemes by which their very wealthy clients, individual or corporate, can evade the laws which are made to regulate in the interest of the public the use of great wealth."

—President Theodore
Roosevelt, 1905

"Support Your Local Lawyer—Send Your Kid to Medical School"

—bumper sticker

"There was a society of men among us, bred up from their youth in the art of proving, by words multiplied for the purpose, that white is black and black is white, according [to] as they are paid."

—*Jonathan Swift, on lawyers, in* Gulliver's Travels

Come to Major Hopkins to get full satisfaction. I win nine-tenths of my cases. If you want to sue, if you have been sued, I am the man to take *your case.* Embezzlement, highway robbery, felonious assault, arson, and horse stealing don't amount to shucks if you have a good lawyer behind you. My strong point is ▷

weeping as I appeal to the jury, and I seldom fail to clear my man. Out of eleven murder cases last year I cleared nine of the murderers. Having been in jail no less than four times myself, my experience cannot fail to prove of value to my clients. Come early and avoid the rush.

—*advertisement for Arizona lawyer Major Hopkins, circa 1895*

"The law is the only profession which records its mistakes carefully, exactly as they occurred, and yet does not identify them as mistakes."

—*Eliot Dunlap Smith*

"Every man in the community owes a duty to our profession; somewhere between the cradle and the grave he must acknowledge the liability and pay the debt. . . . It was one of the brightest members of the profession, you remember, who had taken his passage for Europe . . . and failed to go. He said one of his rich clients died and he was afraid if he had gone across the Atlantic, the heirs would have gotten all the property."

—*Joseph H. Choate*

"No one can have been for twenty years in active and varied legal practice without becoming convinced that the profession to▷

which he belongs harbors within itself examples of as base, deliberate, and ingenious depravity as any that, less favored by fortune or cunning, have gravitated into the penitentiary."

—*Theodore Bacon, 1882*

A LEGAL LIGHTNING BOLT!

"I feel like an idiot, I really do. . . . when it comes down to money they'll just turn around and stab you in the back. . . . Maybe I was deceiving myself; they'd always portrayed themselves as something other than the factory I guess they are."

—*a young Manhattan lawyer, on being laid off by his firm*

"How do you get along at the office? Do you trust each other? Or does each have a separate safe for his money?"
—*Groucho Marx, to lawyer Joseph Welch after seeing the long list of attorneys on the firm's stationery*

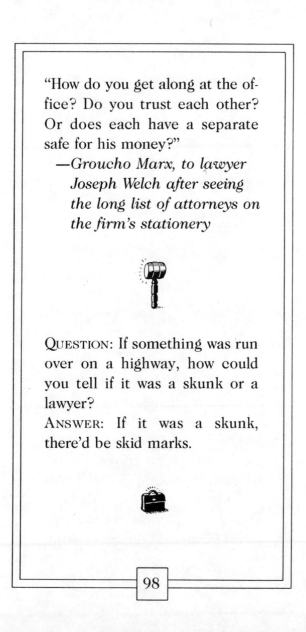

QUESTION: If something was run over on a highway, how could you tell if it was a skunk or a lawyer?
ANSWER: If it was a skunk, there'd be skid marks.

Ugh! The United States is home to two-thirds of the world's lawyers.

After the 30-year-old lawyer died he screamed at Saint Peter, "How can you do this to me? A heart attack at my age! I'm only thirty!"

Replied Saint Peter, "Well, when we looked at your total billable hours, we figured you had to be at least ninety-five."

Beneath this smooth stone by
    the bone of his bone
Sleeps Master John Gill;
By lies when alive this attorney
    did thrive,
And now that he's dead he lies
    still.
    —*epitaph, Massachusetts
    churchyard*

Here lies an honest lawyer,
And that is Strange.
    —*epitaph for the lawyer Sir
    John Strange*

A lawyer died and immediately went to hell for his many professional sins. As the Devil was leading him deeper and deeper into hell, closer and closer to the hottest fires, he noticed another lawyer making passionate love to an absolutely gorgeous woman.

"Damn it," said the lawyer, "how come I'm going to go down even farther to roast forever while this lawyer gets his eternal way with that beautiful woman?"

The Devil turned to him and angrily screamed, "And who are you to question that woman's punishment?!"

GET YOUR NAME IN A BOOK!
SHOW IT OFF TO FRIENDS
AND RELATIVES!

Submit your favorite lawyer item—quotation, anecdote, fact, joke, etc.—for possible publication in *More Lawyers & Other Reptiles*. If the submission is used, you will receive credit *and* a free copy of the new book. (Do not clear this with your lawyer! Save yourself $200! The author can be trusted—he's not a lawyer!) Submit to:

More Lawyers & Other Reptiles
201 West Street
Reading, MA 01867

Note: submissions entered on legal-sized paper will **not** be considered. Not at all!